NATASHA'S WORDS FOR LOVERS

NATASHA JOSEFOWITZ

DRAWINGS BY
MARY MIETZELFELD

D1304362

WARNER BOOKS

A Warner Communications Company

This book is part of a trilogy. The other two
by the same author are:

Natasha's Words for Friends
Natasha's Words for Families

Copyright © 1986 by Natasha Josefowitz
Warner Books, Inc., 666 Fifth Avenue, New York, NY 10103

W A Warner Communications Company

Printed in the United States of America
First Printing: November 1986
10 9 8 7 6 5 4 3 2
Cover design by Mary Mietzelfeld

Library of Congress Cataloging-in-Publication Data

Josefowitz, Natasha.
  Natasha's words for lovers.

  1. Love poetry, American.   I. Title.
PS3560.0768N36   1986   811'.54   86-9250
ISBN 0-446-38299-X (U.S.A.) (pbk.)
     0-446-38300-7 (Canada) (pbk.)

The Poetry of Natasha

"Witty and pithy, like a haiku that lingers in
the mind long after it has been read."
— Ken Wood, *San Francisco Examiner*

"Every minute you spend with Natasha gives
you laughter, pleasure and new insights."
— Spencer Johnson, M.D., co-author
of *The One Minute Manager* and
author of *One Minute for Myself*

"Her voice is filled with clear observation
and hot emotion."
— Adele M. Scheele, Ph.D., author of
Skills for Success

"Natasha Josefowitz's gentle and funny
poetry sneaks its way into our hearts the
way subtle humor does: it's an aesthetic
where the laughter of recognition comes
first and the tears of remembrance come
later — which makes it possible to learn and
be free again."
— Warren Bennis, Joseph Debell
Chair of Management,
University of Southern California

"Natasha Josefowitz, one of the America's
most gifted poets, helps you to reach the
love in your life. She writes with the humor
and the irony that has us laughing together,
leaving us with the insight that men can
hear because it not only rings true but
comes from love."
— Warren Farrell, author of
The Liberated Male
and *Why Men Are The Way They Are*

Also by Natasha Josefowitz

IS THIS WHERE I WAS GOING? *
              (light verse)
PATHS TO POWER: A Woman's Guide
              from First Job to Top
              Executive
YOU'RE THE BOSS! A Guide to
              Managing People with
              Understanding and
              Effectiveness *

*published by Warner Books.

To Herman Gadon. Whereas most muses in antiquity have been women, my muse is today's man, bravely struggling with the new roles, new responsibilities and expectations, without models or precedents. Thank you for the availability, the thoughtfulness, the support and especially the unwavering caring.

Special thanks to Erving Polster and Mort Shaevitz for listening to the poems and giving helpful suggestions, and to the San Diego Authors' Group, who shared their work and their knowledge with each other every month and who, over the years, have given encouragement when needed and celebrated one another's successes.

While some of the verses are autobiographical, many reflect the feelings and experiences of friends and colleagues. I am grateful for their sharing them with me and making this book richer.

Contents

Introduction   xiii

Pretzels in the Night   1

In My Bed   2

Promises   3

One Moment   4

Conundrums   5

The Whole Is More Than The Sum of Its
  Parts   6

My Husband, the Helper   8

I Think You're Wonderful   9

Meet Me at the Street Corner   10

Travel   12

Homecoming   13

Lies?   14

Daily Rediscovery   16

Re-Prioritizing   17

Sins of Omission   18

The New Relationship   19

The Difference Between Men and
  Women   20

A Man's Lot   22

He Worries   23

Before and After   24

Agendas   26

Stages of Marriage   27

Needed: Mutual Support   28

I Don't Love Him Anymore   29

I Knew You Before I Knew You   30
Losing Him   31
Different Tunes   32
Alimony   33
Her Former Husband   34
Divorce   35
New Directions   36
Competition   38
Men Talk/Women Talk   39
Time For Love?   40
The Truth   41
Feeling Close   42
Christmas Day   43
Rye Twist   44
Misunderstandings   45
Jack of All Trades, Master of All   46
The Shapes of Love   52
Man/Child   53
Prejudices   54
Signs in the Sandbox?   55
Clothes   56
Double Standards   57
Ask Me, Don't Tell Me   58
Needed: Body Parts   59
Missed Connections   60
Homo Erectus   61
The Real Difference Between Men and
    Women   62
Body Hunger   63

Sleeping Together   64
Different Pleasures   65
Fantasies   66
Kinky Sex   67
Music   68
You Turn Me On   70
Lust   71
Some of the People Fooling Around   72
A Warning to Men   73
Good Sex   74
Biology   75
Roles   76
Just a Little Fun   77
"If"   78
What's in a Name?   80
Coming on Too Strong   82
Who Is Seducing Whom?   83
No Competition   84
Pygmalion   86
Top Executive   87
Dealing with Her Success   88
I'm Grateful for the Little Things   90
The Best of Times   91
Colors   92
Remember   94
A Huggle   96

Introduction

Only if we can share our hopes and fears,
our secret wishes and hidden vulnerabilities,
so that to each the other is not a mystery
can we accept each other as we are: men
and women, each with our idiosyncracies,
funny little habits, unpleasant quirks and
endearing ways.

It is my hope that these few verses will help
us to look at ourvelves and at each other
with a smile of recognition and
understanding.

Pretzels in the Night

He coils around me
like a pretzel
his limbs so entwined with mine
that it's confusing
whose is which
and so we sleep
turning together
during the night
unwinding to rewind again
curves into hollows
filling empty spaces

I love pretzels.

In My Bed

It's a wondrous thing
a warm, glowing feeling
all over
Every evening as I go to sleep
every morning as I awaken
you are the miracle in my bed.

Promises

I will love you
forever

our forever may be
only today

and I worry about
your tomorrows

for it takes courage
to love a mortal

One Moment

One moment
on a sofa
we are
two strangers

we can talk about
the latest movie
the newest novel
or the last trip

One moment
on a sofa
can be nothing

OR

we can talk about
your worries
my family
our hopes

and in one moment
on a sofa
each can touch
the other's life.

Conundrums

I can't allow myself to be known
unless I can trust the man I'm with
I can't trust him
unless I know him
I can't know him
until I know how he responds to me
he won't know how to respond
until he knows me
But
he can't allow himself to be known
unless he can trust the woman he's with
he can't trust me
unless he knows me
he can't know me
until he knows how I respond to him
I won't know how to respond
until I know him
But
we can't allow ourselves to be
                    known . . .

The Whole Is More Than The Sum of Its Parts

Of course I love you
and I love me too
but most of all
I love "us"

I love the "we"
the you *and* me,
the relationship,
the way each one
is enriched
by the other

I am smarter
when you're around
you are braver
when I am there

We find each other
beautiful, brilliant
and great fun

Each of us is the other's parent
each, the other's child
each is the other's partner, colleague
friend, consultant, lover
and accomplice

You tend to be serious
I'm rather spontaneous
you make me think more
I make you laugh more

Of course I love you
and I love me too
but most of all
I love "us."

My Husband, the Helper

When he cooks
he asks where the pots are

When he vacuums
he does not see the dirt

When he dresses the baby
he asks what she should wear

When he chops the onions
I say thank you

When I cook the dinner
he just eats it

When he markets
it's with my list

When he says he loves me
none of this matters

I Think You're Wonderful

You are intelligent and loving
fun to be with
and always there

you're understanding
and sympathetic
always giving me good advice

you are sensitive
and very honest
and always trying to be fair

you are aware
of today's issues
and always know the way I feel

you're wise and kind
you're wonderful
yet what I like best about you
is that you think
I'm wonderful too.

Meet Me at the Street Corner

We were to meet at this corner
but he's not here.
Am I too early
or is he late?
Perhaps this wasn't the place?
nor the time?
nor even the day?
A tightening in my stomach
I should have repeated
the directions once more
If I look for a phone
he might come
and not find me
and leave
and then I won't know
that he has come and gone
and I could stand here all day
How long should I wait?
Has he forgotten
or had an emergency
or become ill?
I sway between anger
and worry
I hope he's sick
How can I say that?
No, I hope he forgot
How could he do that?
Shall I give up and leave?

Is he standing
at some other corner
worrying
and waiting for me?

Travel

When she takes a trip away from home
she prepares his meals ahead of time
and leaves them in the freezer
with little notes on how to cook
and what to eat when

She calls the laundry about his shirts
a cleaning lady about the house
the friends who might invite him
the neighbors who can look in
she leaves instructions and reminders
and promises to call every day

When he takes a trip away from home
he just packs and leaves.

Homecoming

When he comes home
after a long trip
he wants her right away.
She wants to talk first.

He needs to reconnect
through his body.
She needs to reconnect
the sharing of feelings.

When he comes home
after a long trip
he's hot and quick.
She warms up slowly.

She usually accedes
but she does it for him.
If he would wait
and they could talk
even for just a few minutes

they would be doing it
for each other.

Lies?

I say to him
"Dear, all I want
is to stay home with you"
and I really mean it.

But when I'm called to speak here
or go there
or write this
or do that
I happily accept
go wherever
and do whatever.

And I say to him
"I'm sorry, dear,
I wanted so much
just to stay home with you"
and I really meant it.

I do not know
which is the truth:
what I say
or what I do?

Daily Rediscovery

Each morning
as we awaken
we rediscover
each other
with the same
delight
and the same
surprise

Re-Prioritizing

Most often I choose work
feeling there's no alternative . . .
like a mortgage and
grocery bills.

Sometimes I choose the children
feeling an obligation
to spend time with them
take them somewhere
read them a story.

Seldom do I choose you
feeling that love can wait
when in fact it will not
and should take first priority
every single day.

Sins of Omission

It is not only what I say
for I am seldom prejudiced
in any obvious way

It is what I don't say:
the forgetting
the not noticing
the disregarding
the overlooking

It is not only the support not given
it is not knowing
when it is needed

I do not sin by commission anymore
I sin by omission.

The New Relationship

He knows my most intimate thoughts
he reads all my letters
helps with my writing
figures out my income tax.

He is there early in the morning
greeting me with a smile
he is waiting for me late at night
ready to do my bidding.

We play games together,
do puzzles, paint pictures,
when I can't find something
he helps me search for it.

He always warns me
of impending problems
and tells me how to fix them
never impatient with my mistakes.

He is my newest love
available, dependable and friendly,
gets turned on at the flick of my finger,
and never tires of performing.

There are many parts to him
including a charming electronic accent
and so we have become inseparable
my new computer and I.

The Difference Between Men and Women

He does not suffer a sleepless night
worrying whether he picked the right color
to reupholster the sofa

He does not feel guilty
when he breaks the diet
he is supposed to be on
for the rest of his life

He does not have a stomachache
because his daughter is unhappy
in her current relationship

He is not depressed
because he had a slight argument
over nothing
with his wife

He does not think it's his duty
to cook a meal
for a sick friend

He does not feel responsible
that it rains
when there are weekend guests

He does not believe
he is a total failure
because one thing went wrong

I do!

A Man's Lot

He comes home late every night
tired from his day at work
the kids are already asleep
If only he could have kissed them good night

He would like to stay home
but she's been in all day
and wants to get out of the house

They have friends to see
and errands to do
and things that need to get fixed

She's upset with him
because he works too hard
and has no time for her, for the children

He's upset with her
for not understanding
that he knocks himself out for them all

He Worries

He's worried about the mortgage
but doesn't want to tell her

He's anxious about the car payments
but doesn't want her to know

He's losing on the stock market
but won't burden her with it

He may not get his promotion
but is afraid to tell her

He's not sure of his performance
but is ashamed to share this with her

So if he's quiet
and seems preoccupied
it is not because
he doesn't love her

Before and After

During their courtship
he talked a lot
about his hopes, fears
and expectations
he shared his feelings
and expressed emotions

During their courtship
she listened to him
was very warm
and very loving
and spent hours telling him
how wonderful he was

He was thrilled
to be marrying
such a passionate woman

She was thrilled
to be marrying
a man who could communicate

After the wedding
he worked very hard
came home tired
read the paper
and didn't want to talk

After the wedding
she became harried
was always exhausted
watched TV
and didn't want sex

If she just put
her arms around him
and he just told her
how he felt

they could find
each other again.

Agendas

Saturday: he worked hard all week
now wants to relax
she's folding the laundry
he suggests doing something fun together
she's doing something in the kitchen
he watches TV feeling lonesome
she's putting clothes away
he doesn't feel like pitching in
she wishes that he did
he wants to go out
and needs her company
she needs to stay in
and wants his help
he's lonely and guilty
she's lonely and angry
for this is his day to wind down
but this is her day to catch up.

Stages of Marriage

In the first years of their marriage
when the children are small
and she's into formulas and diapers
and getting up at night
and he's just at the beginning of his career
he wants sex
but she's too exhausted

In the middle years of their marriage
when the children are older
and he's into vice-presidencies
and travel on business
and she finally has some time
she wants sex
but he's too exhausted

In the last years of their marriage
when they both have slowed down
and they're finally in sync
both get what they want
and sex is great.

Needed: Mutual Support

She came home
after a bad day at the office
needing his support
a cup of hot tea
and reassurance
but she didn't tell him that

He also had a rough day
needed a listener
a neck rub
and some compassion
but he didn't say that

so instead
they had a fight.

I Don't Love Him Anymore

I told myself,
I don't love him anymore
he hurt me
I hope he's hurting too
I hope he suffers
terribly

And then I saw his face
drawn with exhaustion and pain
and felt worse
about *his* suffering
than about mine

Maybe I love him still?

I Knew You
Before I Knew You

Even before I knew you
I was looking for you
so that when I met you
I recognized you
as having existed
within me
as far back
as I can remember
And now that I know
you are here
not only in my wishes
but in reality
I can let go of dreaming
and celebrate each day.

Losing Him

Losing him
is not only
losing a lover
it is losing
a friend
a colleague
a mentor
a parent
it is losing
a way of life

though it is hard to believe right now
a new way of life
is waiting
to be found

Different Tunes

She sings:
"Someday my prince
will come"
and she dreams
of tenderness
and a long life together

He sings:
"There is nothing like a dame"
and dreams
of quickies
here today, gone tomorrow

Alimony

She wishes
Her first husband
Would pay her alimony

She wishes
Her second husband
Would not pay alimony
To his first wife.

Her Former Husband

He used to fit
like an old shoe
it wasn't his fault
that her feet grew
the shoes became too tight
her feet felt constrained
she tried to get the shoes to stretch
but they couldn't
or they wouldn't

A cobbler tried to stretch them too
but her husband liked being
that same old shoe
when her toes became too cramped
she chose to go barefoot.

Divorce

The one who has been left
feels rejected
and asks questions that have
no answers.

The one who leaves
feels guilty
and answers questions
that no one asks.

New Directions

She has not been taught
how to fix a car
   He has not been taught
   how to follow a recipe

She has not learned
how to fix a leaky faucet
   He has not learned
   how to sew on a loose button

She wishes she had more time
for outside activities
   He wishes he had more time
   for his family

She feels tied down
by the children
   He feels tied down
   by his job

If she's successful
she is unfeminine
   If he's not successful
   he's not masculine

She wishes she could
show her anger
      He wishes he could
      show his feelings

She wants sometimes
to be allowed to lead
      He wants sometimes
      to be allowed to follow

She doesn't want to pretend
vulnerability when she's strong
      he doesn't want to pretend
      strength when he's vulnerable

She wants to earn
as much as he does
      He's tired of being
      the main support

It's time for her
to learn more about the world
      It's time for him
      to learn more about himself

Competition

If I think
I am better than you
and you think
you are smarter than I
we will spend
a lot of time
trying to persuade
each other
of our particular
superiority

Time
we can spend better
discovering
each other

Men Talk/Women Talk

It used to be
that men talked of
the latest deal,
politics, sports, cars

And women talked
of children,
recipes and life

I yearned for the day
when women would talk of business
                    opportunities
and men of interpersonal relationships

And now that it has happened
I don't like it any better
than the other way around.

Time For Love?

Women make love
When they feel good

Men make love
To feel good!

The Truth

She loves him because
She knows him so well

She loves him in spite of
knowing him that well

Feeling Close

I like it best
when we can be
together in a car
not being entertaining
not making conversation
not talking at all

silently intimate.

Christmas Day

In New York it broke all records
a balmy 54
you went out in short sleeves
basking in the sun

on the same day in California
it dipped to 54
I put on a sweater
and shivered in the cold

We live in different places now
so far away, so out of touch
Just because we react to
the same weather differently
does not mean
we're less in love

Rye Twist

When he is the sole breadwinner
she is the sole bread baker
and that's her duty

When she becomes the breadwinner too
he learns to bake bread
but that's his hobby.

Misunderstandings

He believes
he works so hard
for her

She suspects
he works so hard
because he loves it.

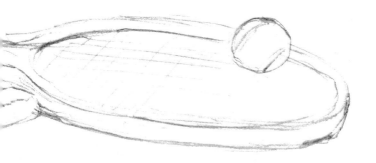

Jack of All Trades, Master of All

I'm a man of today
I know exactly what's expected of me
I should be tall, athletic
have broad shoulders and narrow hips
have a nice tan and wear
French bikini underwear

I should work, be successful,
earn a good living in order to provide
home, cars and private schools

I should also be able to
spend time with my family,
fix things around the house,
coach the Little League games
and go to parents' day

I should be well read,
up with the latest,
in with the crowd,
lots of fun, a good listener,
tender and caring

I'm supposed to be in charge,
yet follow her decisions
I should love music, the ballet,
be a good dancer
and not drink too much

I should always be the driver,
open doors, light cigarettes,
pay for dinners, but do it all
so that she doesn't feel
she couldn't do it too

I should never say mankind, policeman
fireman or mailman
but talk of humanity, police officers
fire fighters and mail carriers
I should say he-or-she,
women instead of girls
and never laugh at sexist jokes

I shouldn't comment on a woman's body
nor guess at her measurements
nor wonder out loud
what she's like in bed
I am to be able to turn women on
but be faithful to one
get it up on command
and keep it up forever

I should see women as equals
even prefer a female boss
wish for a woman President
share equally in the household chores
be a gourmet cook
and know how to clean a bathroom

I should be able to
sew a loose button,
plan for a party, change a diaper
call my mother-in-law
and represent my company
at the next regional conference

I should be upwardly mobile
inwardly reflective
in touch with my feelings
able to express them appropriately,
have strong opinions
but be open to suggestions,
decisive but flexible
caring yet strong

I should be hardheaded
but softhearted,
show affection in public
exercise regularly, play sports
eat sensibly, not smoke,
talk in bed for hours
making passionate love
while preparing the next day's
financial report

I should not be afraid of intimacy
vulnerability or commitments,
include women
in my old boys' network
campaign for the ERA
read Betty Friedan and Gloria Steinem
and subscribe to *MS.* magazine

I must proclaim myself a feminist
believe in the right to choose
be neither sexist nor racist
with my consciousness raised

I'm a man of today
I'm the man of the future

And if at first
I don't succeed
I'll try, try
again.

The Shapes of Love

You are my pyramid
solid as the Rock of Gibraltar
you are straight as an arrow
yet all angles at times
you can also be a square
you draw circles around me
together we are yin and yang
our love has no boundaries
it is infinite

Geometry!

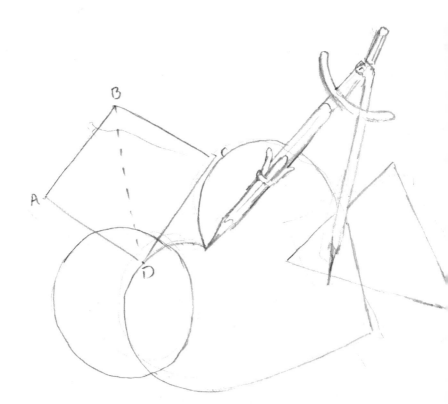

Man/Child

He called
said he wasn't
feeling well

a headache
a backache
a sore throat
a fever

couldn't I please
come home?

I suggested two aspirins
a cup of hot tea
but no, there was this little boy
begging for *me*

and so I went home
to hold his hand
take his temperature
stroke his head

make him soup
feel sorry for him
and stay by his side
so that he could get well
my little boy
of fifty-five

Prejudices

Gay

not black
not Catholic
not Jewish
not old
not poor
not obese
without an accent
yet unacceptable

Gay

too different
Or not different enough?

Signs in the Sandbox?

If she climbs trees
it's cute
and it will pass

If he likes dolls
it's a worry
Will he be gay?

Clothes

Why is it that
when women wear
men's clothes
they're chic?

But when men wear
women's clothes
they're not?

Double Standards

Before the wedding:
    She should be a virgin
    and he?
    Well, you know how boys are ...

After the wedding:
    She should be faithful
    and he?
    Well, you know how men are ...

Ask Me, Don't Tell Me

if you ask me softly
how I am
you are just
seeking information

IF YOU TELL ME LOUDLY
HOW I AM
YOU ARE MAKING
AN ACCUSATION

Needed: Body Parts

A brain to pick
A shoulder to cry on
A kick in the pants

A hand to hold
An arm to lean on
And a step to follow

Missed Connections

When he wants it
She doesn't

When she's ready
He can't

Homo Erectus

He says:

"I get an erection
when I hear your name

I get an erection
at the sound of your voice

at the sight of your body

when I gaze at your face

when you come near me

when I can smell you

when I can touch you
I get an erection."

She says:

"Yes, but do you love me?"

The Real Difference Between Men and Women

He likes to be touched
anytime
anywhere
he always likes to be touched
caressed
fondled
he's always ready
always eager

Sometimes she doesn't want
to be touched
hugged, yes
touched, no

He doesn't understand
that sometimes her body
needs to be left alone
but so that he shouldn't feel rejected
she lets him touch her anyway
reluctantly

and then he says
"see, you liked it"
maybe yes,
but maybe no.

Body Hunger

Needing to
feel her breasts against his chest

Needing to
feel her thighs encircling his

Needing to
feel his arms around her tightly

Needing to
feel his hands moving on her body

Needing to
reconfirm that they are one
before they get out of bed
and start their separate days.

Sleeping Together

Sometimes
in the middle of the night
when he comes into her
neither of them
quite awake
nor fast asleep
they link together
in the dark
united
by a bond
far stronger
than the joining of their bodies.

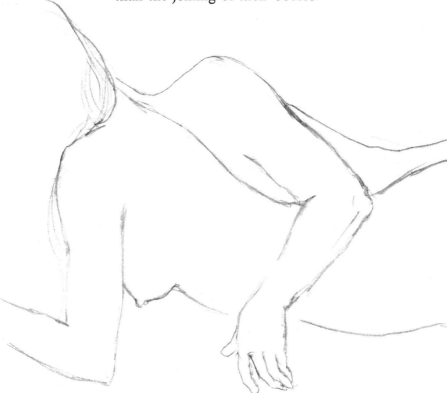

Different Pleasures

Most times
when he makes love to her
she gets excited
responds in kind
and he's delighted

Sometimes
when he makes love to her
it is so soothing
she falls asleep
and he's offended

In fact
it is an equal pleasure
just different from his.

Fantasies

She is the slave of an Arab sheik
who makes wild love to her
in his desert tent

She is a go-go girl
dancing nude
in a Las Vegas bar

She's a prim spinster
carried off
by some primitive man

She's a porn queen
performing in front of
a camera crew

Secret fantasies
are the dreams
that reality
would make
into nightmares.

Kinky Sex

Some do it hanging from chandeliers
others enjoy group sex

Some do it with animals
others like it with drugs

Some do it in strange positions
Others seek exotic settings

Some do it in public places
others prefer it alone

I like to hug and kiss
and talk a lot
about our thoughts and feelings

and do it in the comfort of our bed
when the house is quiet
and the kids are asleep

and then take time
to hug and kiss
and mostly talk a lot.

Music

As she lies next to him
she is his violin
all smooth curves
waiting to be played upon

As he lies next to her
he is her bow
straight and thin
rigidly poised
in expectation

Slowly he fine-tunes her body
listening for the different sounds
their music makes
as his bow glides
over her body

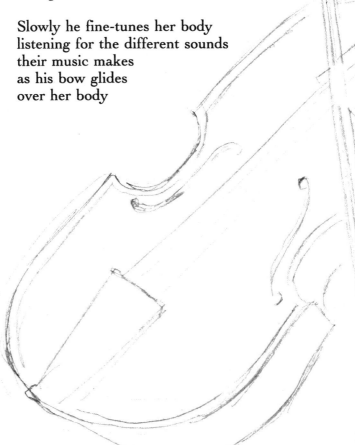

at first tentatively
testing the chords
then gently
plucking at the strings

until the soft humming
becomes a duet
then a string ensemble
and some brass joins in
finally the full orchestra
explodes in a symphony
of cymbals and drums

The applause is silent.

You Turn Me On

You turn me on
not only by what you say
or how you touch me
but by just being you

I look at you
and get turned on
the way you stand
or move or talk

the way you think
the way you look at me
the way you are
turns me on

Lust

He says
she has
a wanton body.

He says
she looks like
she's always
wantin' it.

She says
he's
projecting.

Some of the People Fooling Around

Whereas some women
have sex on their minds
all of the time
and all women have
sex on their minds
some of the time

all men have
sex on their minds
all of the time.

A Warning to Men

Sometimes when she dances
she wiggles her ass
and presses her breasts
against some manly chest
She thrusts her pelvis against his
just for the fun of exciting
but with no intention
of following through

She teases
to please
herself.

Good Sex

The more I give
The more I get

The more I get
The more I want

The more I want
The better it gets

Biology

I have been taught
that the clitoris
is an atrophied penis
that it's a smaller version
of the real thing

Recently, research has shown
that the penis
is an outgrowth
of the clitoris
a longer version
of the initial thing

At last they've got it right!

Roles

Women know who they are
Men know what to do
We need to learn to act
They need to learn to be

Just a Little Fun

The men talk about the women
sexist remarks
about scoring
and measurements

The women gossip about the men
laughing behind their backs
but within hearing distance
ridiculing them

Inside jokes
shared secrets
no harm meant
no pain intended

Yet it hurts
in hidden ways
those at whose expense
we're having
just a little fun.

"If"

If you call her a woman
and not one of the girls

If you write "Dear Sir/Madam"
and not only just "Dear Sir"

If you're not embarrassed
when she pays for dinner

If you do not lose face
when she beats you at tennis

If you seek her opinions
as you would any man's

If you go on a trip
and do not make a pass

If she smiles at you warmly
you don't assume she's "turned on"

If she makes more money
your manhood isn't threatened

If she becomes your boss
you don't find it demeaning

If at her office party
you don't feel out of place

If you're home with sick kids
and don't think it's her job

If she's in the limelight
you do not feel threatened

If you do not laugh
at chauvinist jokes

You're a real man, my friend.

What's in a Name?

A piece of ass
obviously doesn't have a thought in her head

a piece of tail
couldn't harbor a feeling

a lay
doesn't have a first name

a good screw
is all she really is

a chick
you notice but don't talk to

a broad
is good for a laugh

a dame
couldn't have a mind of her own

a girl
can't be taken seriously

a lady
won't let you get close

but a woman
is a man's equal.

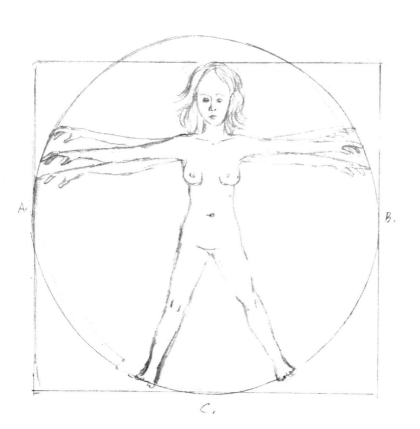

Coming on Too Strong

A party: he's standing alone
with a glass of wine
scanning the room
a woman smiles at him
he nods, not remembering
                    whether he has met her
she comes over and starts a conversation
punctuated by laughter and sexual remarks
he tries to keep up, feeling uncomfortable
she suggests they sit down
she crosses and uncrosses her legs
her skirt creeping up
too high
he looks
then turns away
then looks again
her hand is on his arm
her knee touches his
she's whispering something
he's sweating
not ready to take her on
not willing to let her go
not knowing what to do.

Who Is Seducing Whom?

Is she seducing him
or is he harassing her
who started anyway?
She wears tight sweaters
and giggles at his jokes.
He pats her
you know where
and squeezes
you know what.

First she liked it
now she doesn't.
If she flirts
and he follows through
who is really seducing whom?

No Competition

I have a friend
who has other friends
but I would like to be
her very best friend

I have a teacher
who has other students
but I would like to be
her favorite one

I have a boss
who has other staff members
but I would like him
to trust me the most

I have an editor
who has other authors
but I would like her
to think me the best

I have a doctor
who has other patients
but I would like him
to prefer me to the rest

I have a lawyer
who has other clients
but I would like to be
his most interesting one

I have a mother
who has other children
but I would like to be
the one she loves best

I have grandchildren
who have other grandparents
but I would like them
to love me the most

I have a man
who has no other woman
and I love knowing
that I'm his only love.

Pygmalion

He taught her
everything he knew

and now that she knows
as much as he does

he doesn't like it.

Top Executive

If I want to see my wife
I must make an appointment
through her administrative assistant

her secretary calls me
if my wife will be late

if she has no time to meet me
we'll have a bite in her office
catered by the best restaurant in town

she has her letters typed
her visitors screened
her calls put on hold

she answers the phone during dinner
"only when it's long distance"

she reads long reports at bedtime
only urgent matters of course

At her office party
I'm the tagalong
dismissed as an appendage
with no name of my own
introduced to the group
as the husband of
THE CHIEF EXECUTIVE OFFICER

Dealing with Her Success

His wife is very successful
she earns more money than he does
has a higher position
commands more attention
has perks he does not have
sits on the board of directors
and flies in the corporate jet

He's happy for her
but he's not happy for himself
she used to be *his* wife
now he's just *her* husband

People ask him
what he does
but don't really listen
What they want to know is
how he deals with her success.

He says he doesn't mind
he even says it's wonderful
but he's not telling the truth
because he's ashamed
to be jealous
because he feels guilty
that he's envious
and there is absolutely no one
he can talk to

If he doesn't tell anyone
he'll never find out
that most men
feel the same way.

I'm Grateful for the Little Things

I listen to the silence
I'm grateful that
in our times of noise pollution
I have a quiet room

I breathe the air
I'm grateful that
in our times of air pollution
I have a fragrant garden

When I take a walk
I'm grateful that
I'm not in a car, bus, train or plane
but just on my feet

I eat a plum from our tree
I'm grateful that
it ripened on the branch
with no chemicals added

When I gaze at you
I'm grateful that
in our times of rushing around
I can take time out
take time off
take the time
just to look at you.

The Best of Times

It may not be a perfect time
but it's the best of times
when women can be strong
and not dependent
upon men
to earn a living

We're living in the best of times
when men can be emotional
and not dependent
upon women
to cook and clean and raise their children

We're living in the best of times
when all of us
are free to be whatever
we choose to be.

Colors

You can eat colors
raspberry, cherry, apricot,
plum, orange, grape,
olive and saffron

or adorn yourself with them
turquoise, ruby, emerald,
garnet, aquamarine, gold and silver

or touch a skin color
lily white, ebony, copper, or peaches and
                    cream
hair slides through your fingers
strawberry blond or pepper and salt

You can smell the colors of
lilacs, violets or fuchsias
rose can be dusty or old

and you can drink colors
burgundy, brandy and chocolate

walking in the woods, you find
walnut and mahogany
and touch a whole forest green

Color is not
for the eyes only.

Remember

Remember how
you loved me then
you love me better now

Remember how
we dreamed and planned
we're doing it all now

Remember how
we were so young
we both have wrinkles now

Remember when
the kids were small
grandchildren are here now

Remember how
we used to jog
we smell the flowers now

Remember how
we skiied downhill
we ski cross-country now

Remember how
we ate at Mother's
the kids come to us now

Remember how
we rushed through life
we take our time right now

Remember how
I loved you then
I love you better now.

A Huggle

is a snuggle
and a cuddle
with a hug

Huggles are
the best!